Francis Creek Fjords Coloring Books: Color Your Way Into English Riding 1
ISBN-13: 978-0-9971624-1-7
Copyright © 2016 Francis Creek Fjords, LLC, Francis Creek, WI. All rights reserved.
Published by Francis Creek Fjords (www.FrancisCreekFjords.com). Printed by CreateSpace.

Patti Jo Walter and her husband, Dave Walter, started Francis Creek Fjords (FCF) in 1995. FCF was a Fjord hub for nearly two decades, having Fjords come from all over the United States to be trained, sold on consignment, or bred to their stallion, Fair Acres Ole. Patti Jo began giving riding lessons in 1998, teaching myriad disciplines: huntseat, dressage, jumping, and driving. Today, she continues to instruct dressage and jumping, sharing her passion with anyone wishing to learn and have fun with horses.

Patricia Holland, born and raised in Northeastern Pennsylvania, attended York Academy of Art to pursue a career in commercial art. Dovetailing her lifelong passions of art and horses, she became a professional horse trainer, illustrating what she saw, what she learned, and the people she met along the way. With humor and wit she juggles these contrasting careers, creating a rich and fulfilling life. She resides and illustrates in Galena, Illinois.

Norwegian Fjord Horses (N.F.H.), featured in many of these drawings, are an offshoot horse breed well known for their gentle disposition, calm demeanor, and great versatility, but it's their loving and humorous personalities that draw in most owners. Mutual affection for these charismatic animals caused Pat and Patti's lives to intersect. Once united, Pat's humor and wit served as the perfect complement to Patti's love of life, forging a lifelong friendship in and out of the pasture, much like the horses they admire.

Pat and Patti created this coloring book series as a fun way of learning horseback riding terminology and concepts for Francis Creek Fjords' students. Pat's skillfully drawn illustrations—filled with humor, life, and laughter—combined with Patti's impressive understanding of horses and students resulted in a colorful array of barnyard characters teaching valuable horse-related lessons you can color.

How to use this book

Step 1: Grab your crayons or colored pencils! (Markers are not recommended)

....

Step 2: Choose your favorite picture!

....

Step 3: Color!

....

Step 4: Have fun!

....

Don't forget to read the notes and study the images. There are lessons to be learned within these pages.

So You Want to Ride a Horse?

Here's What You Need to Know

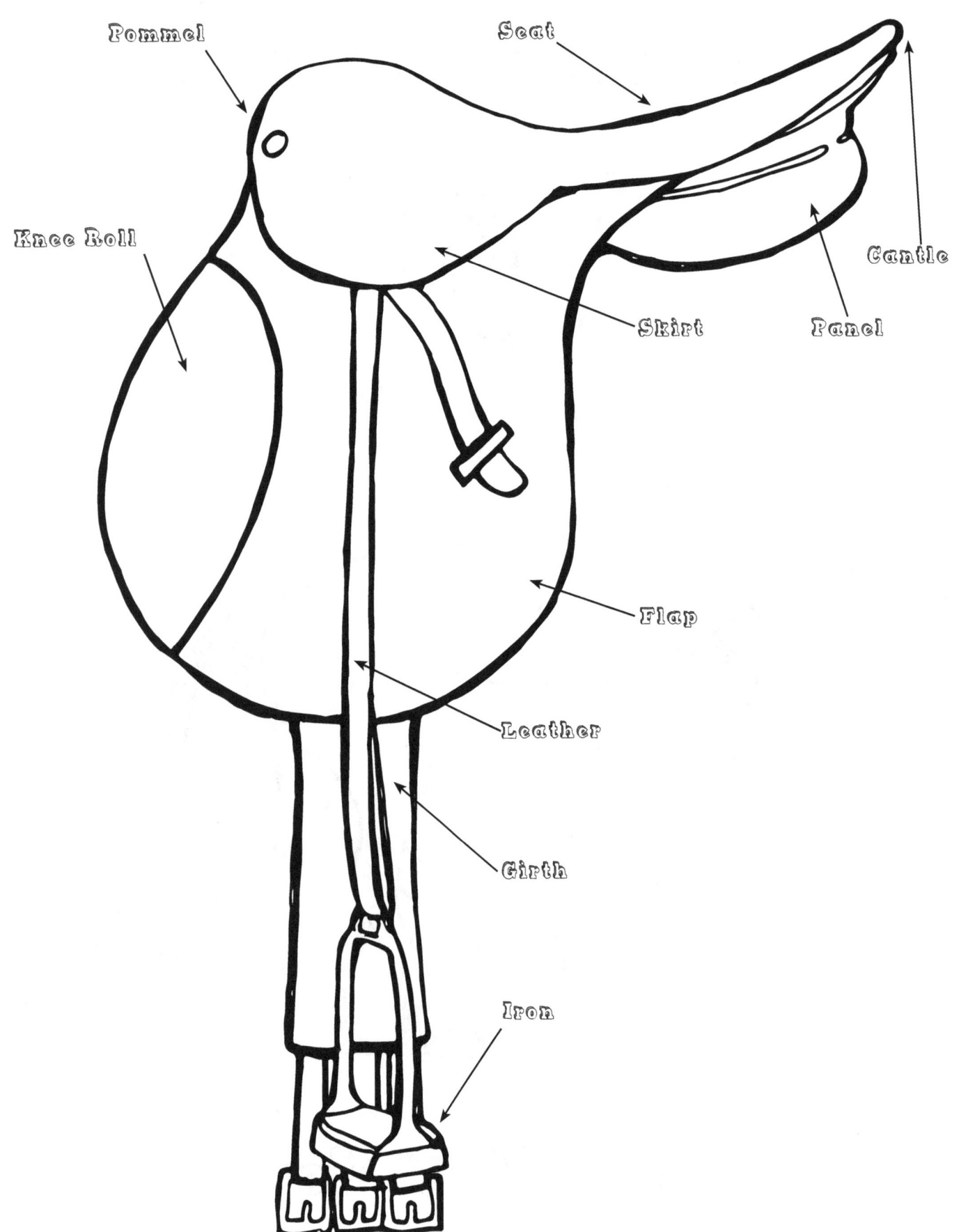

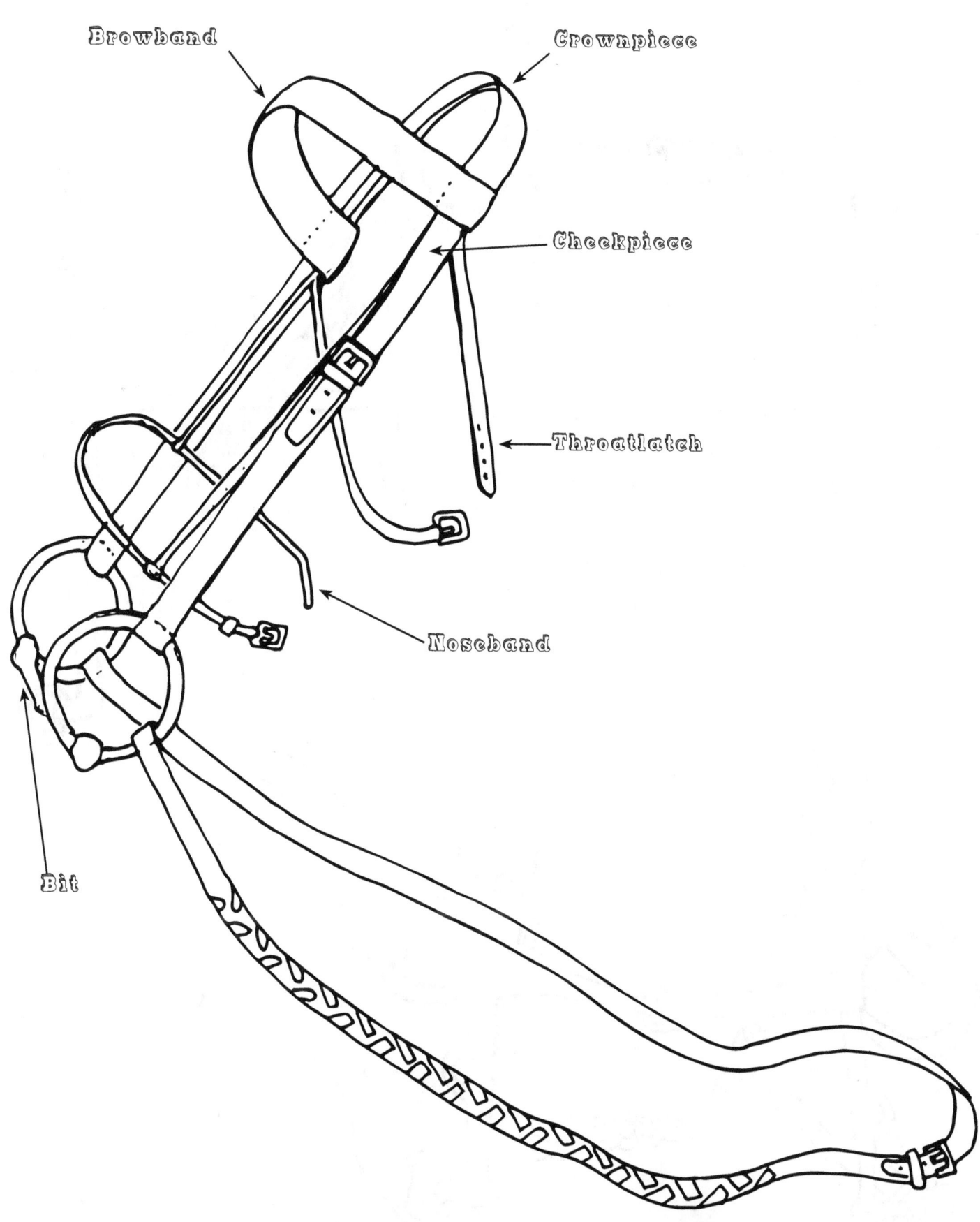

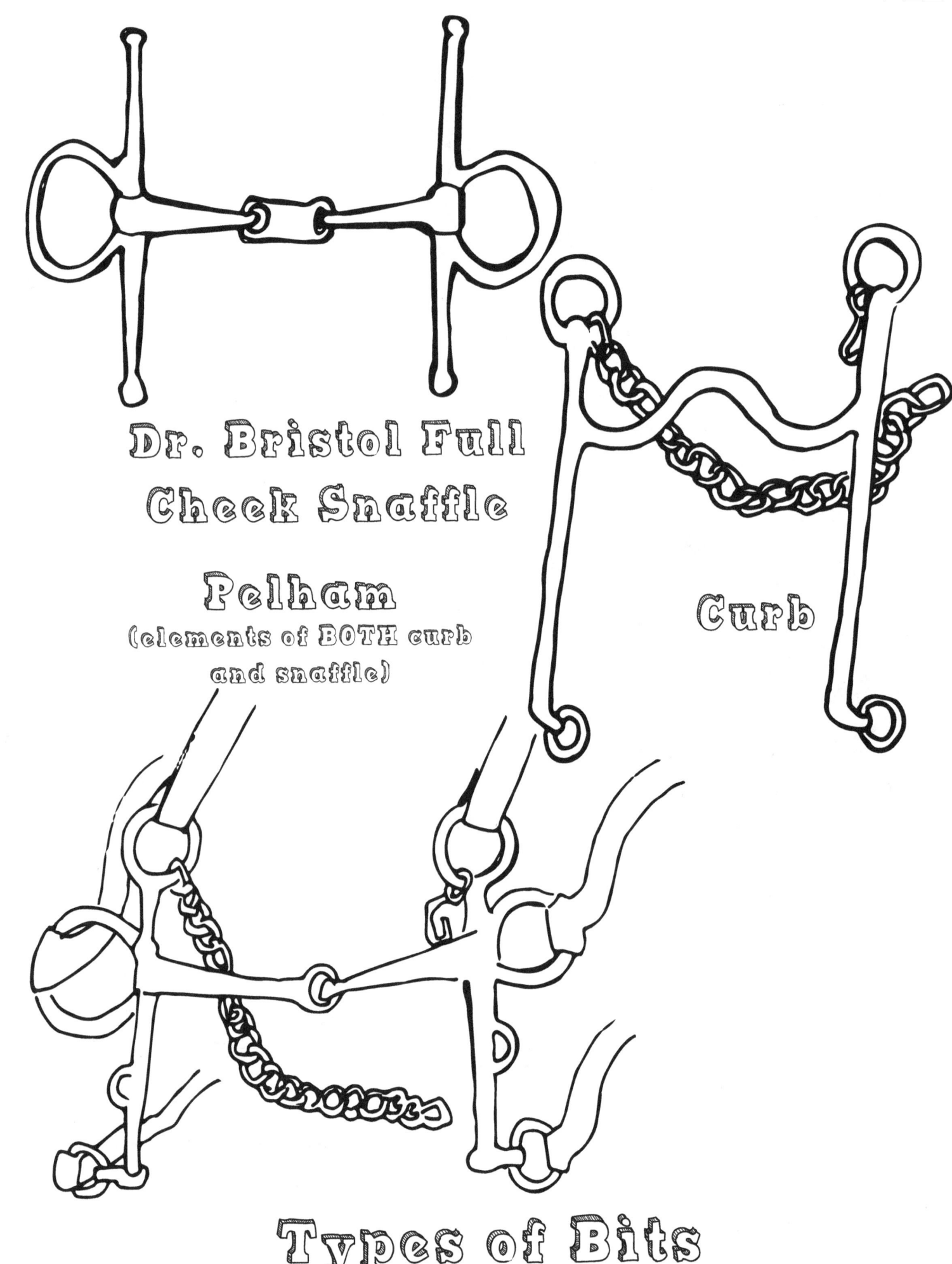

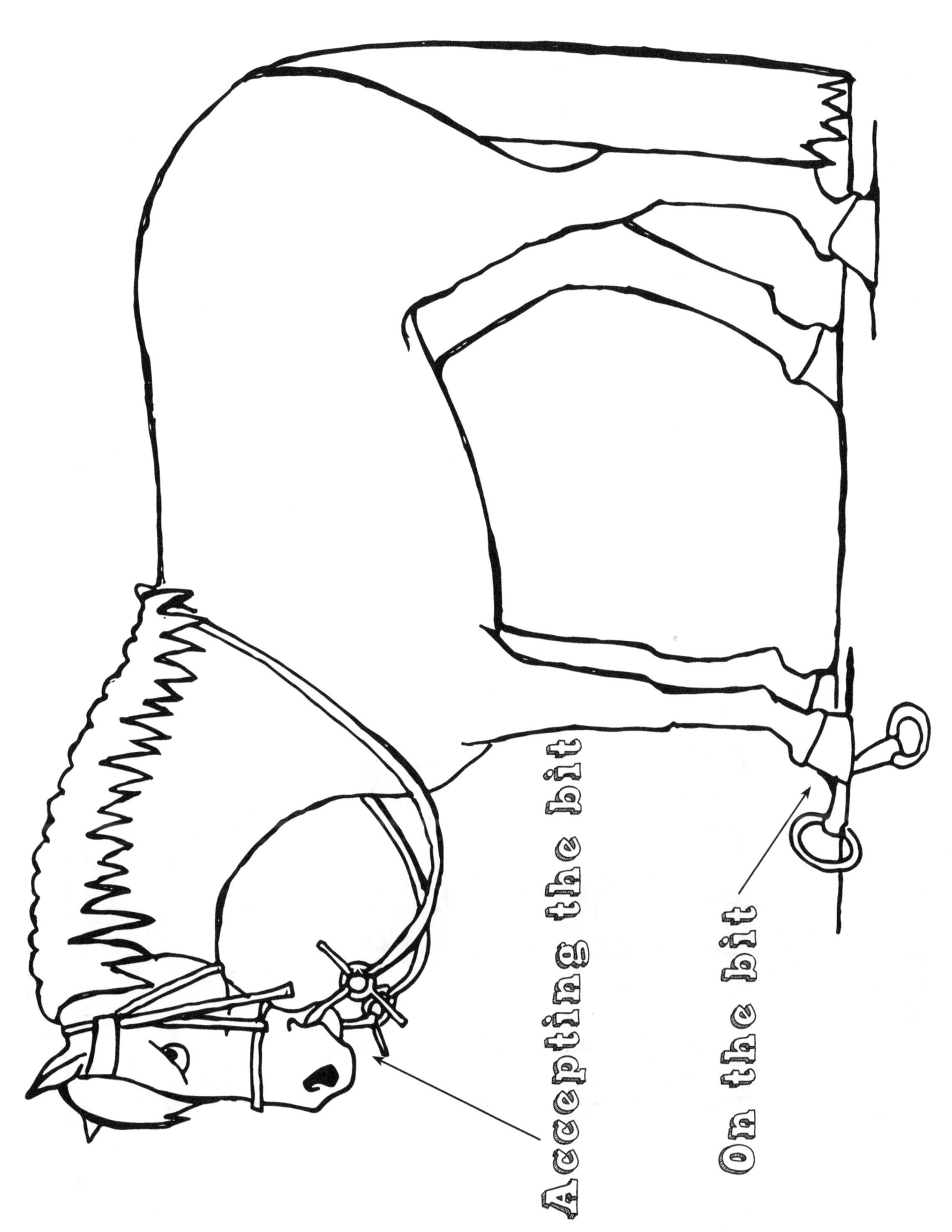

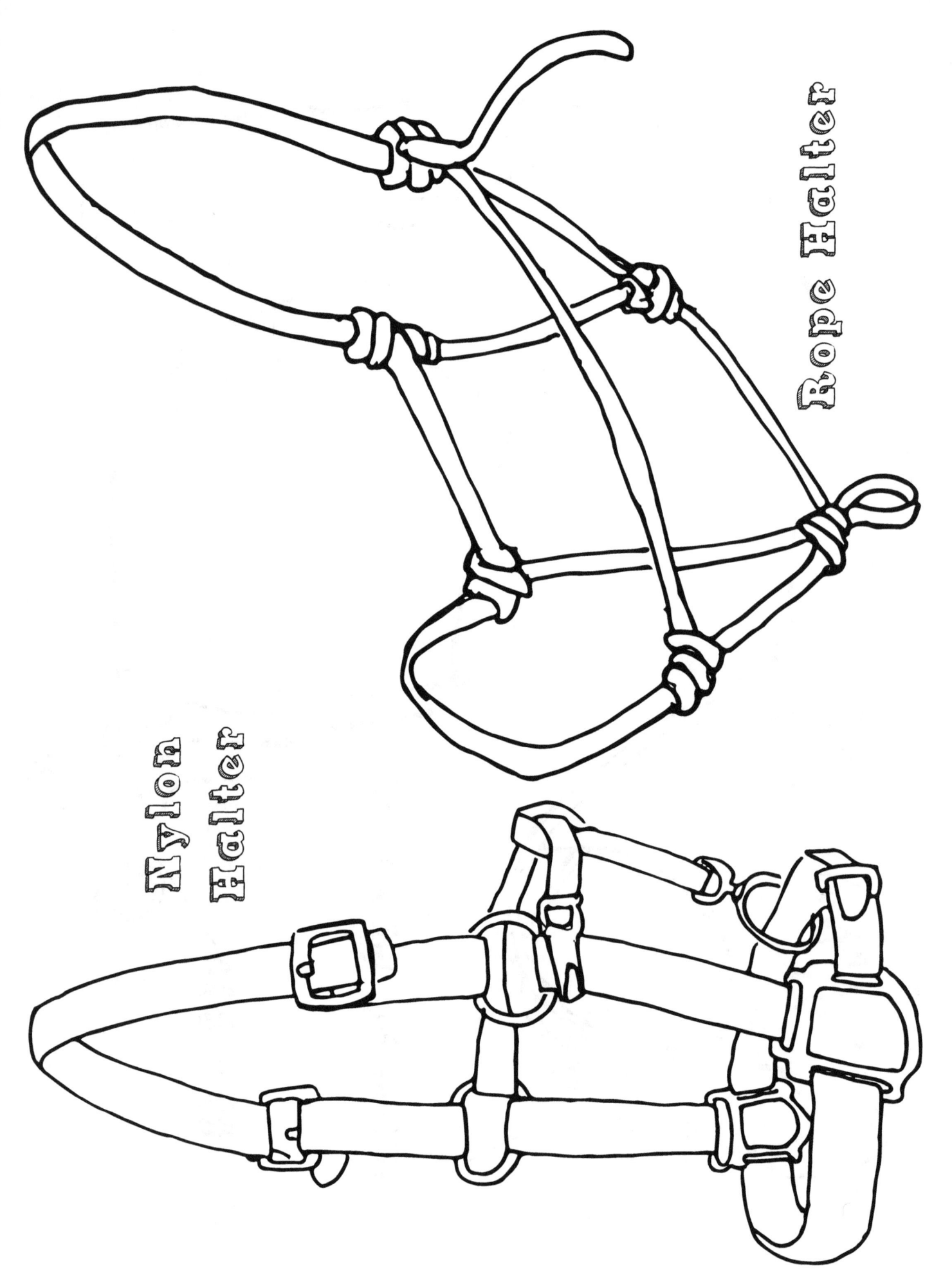

Hunt Seat Attire   Eventing Attire

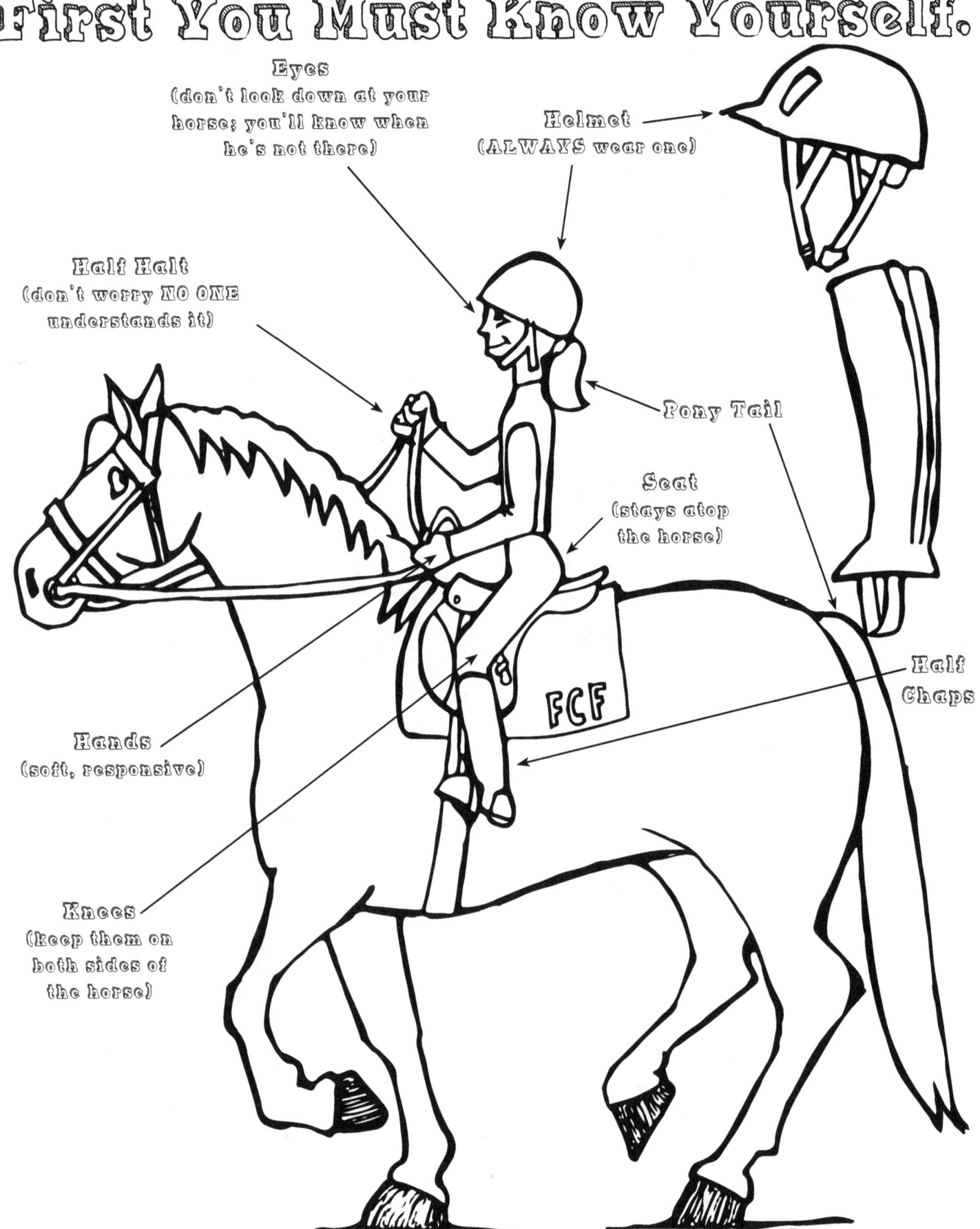

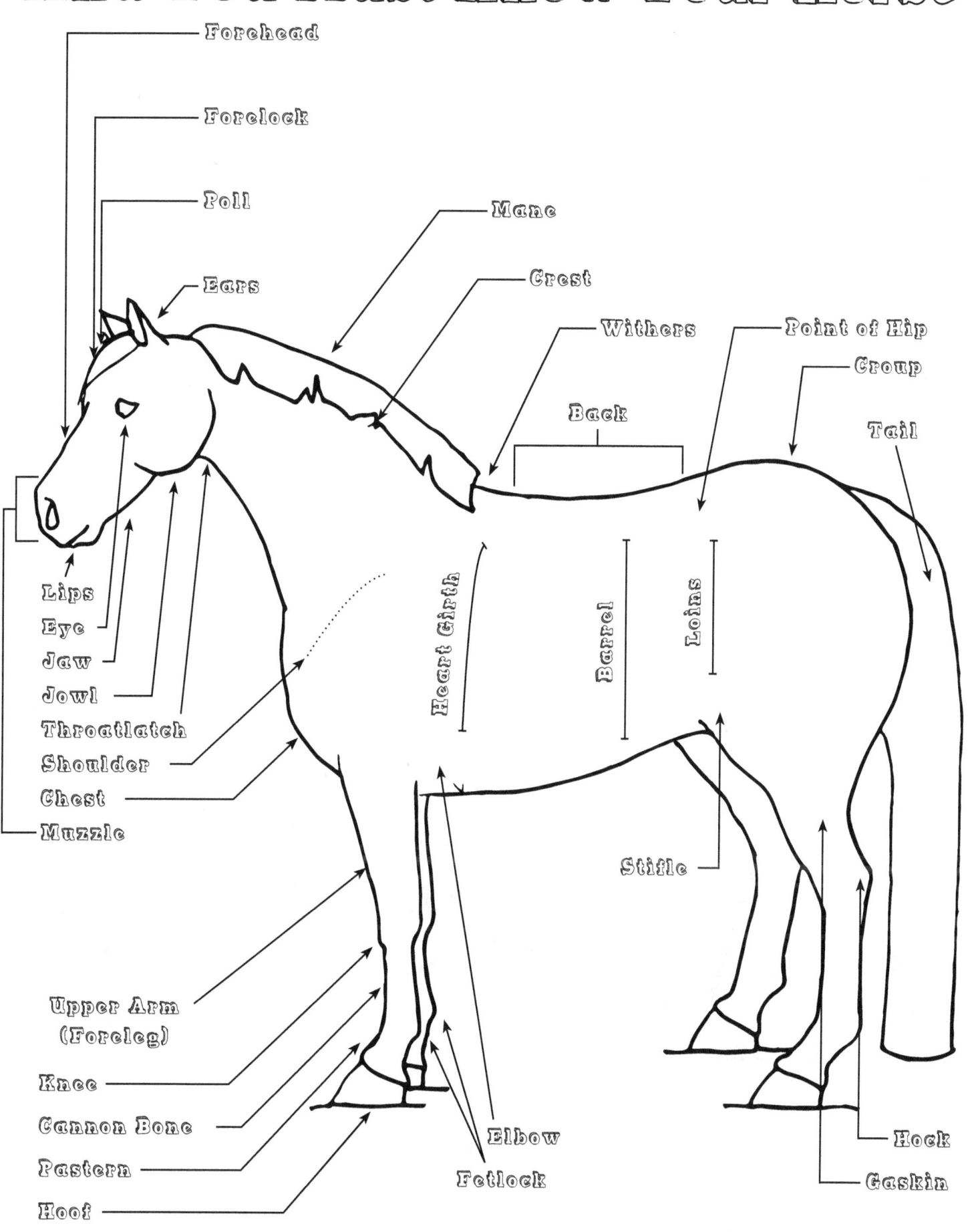

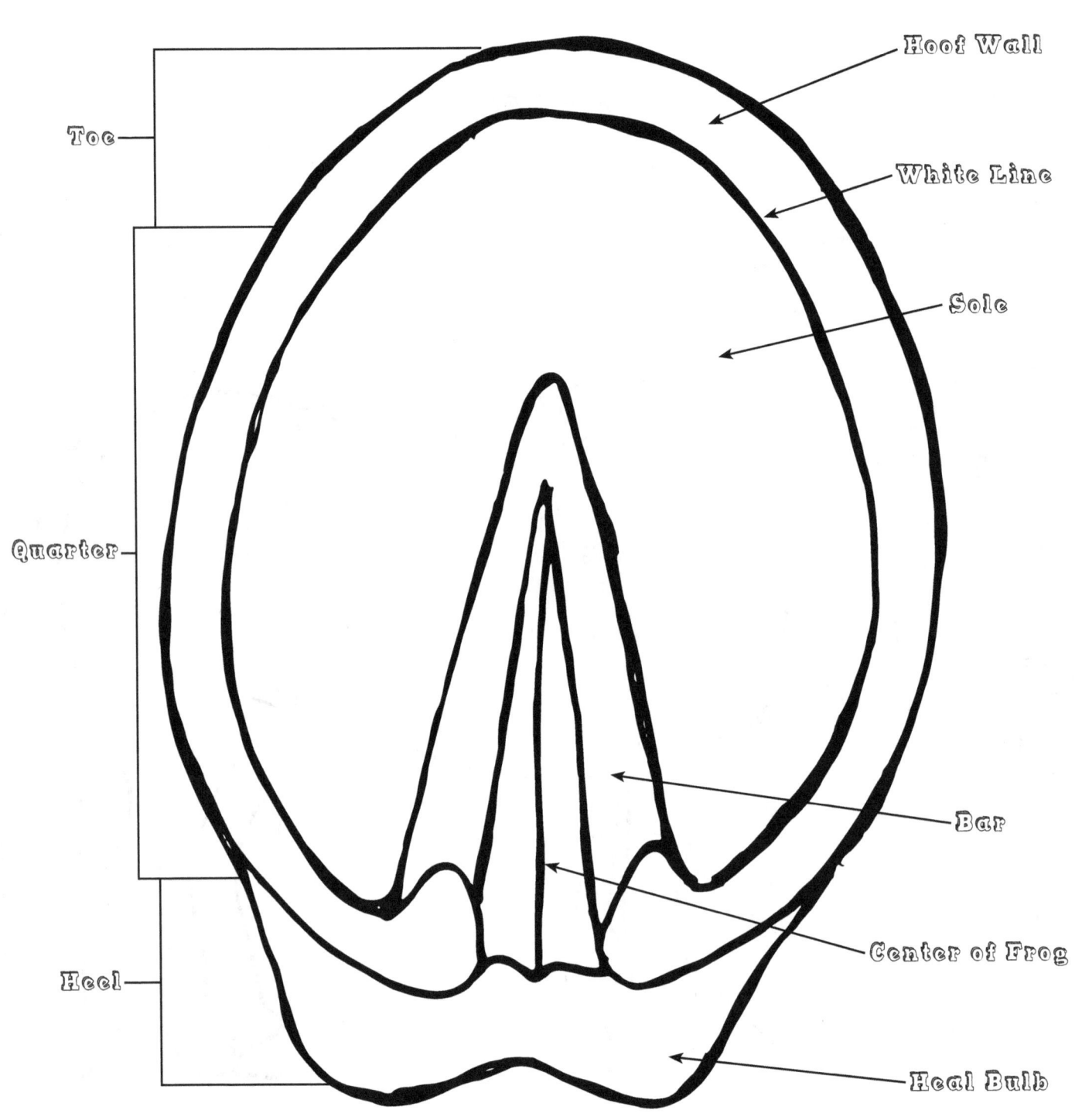

Parts of a Hoof

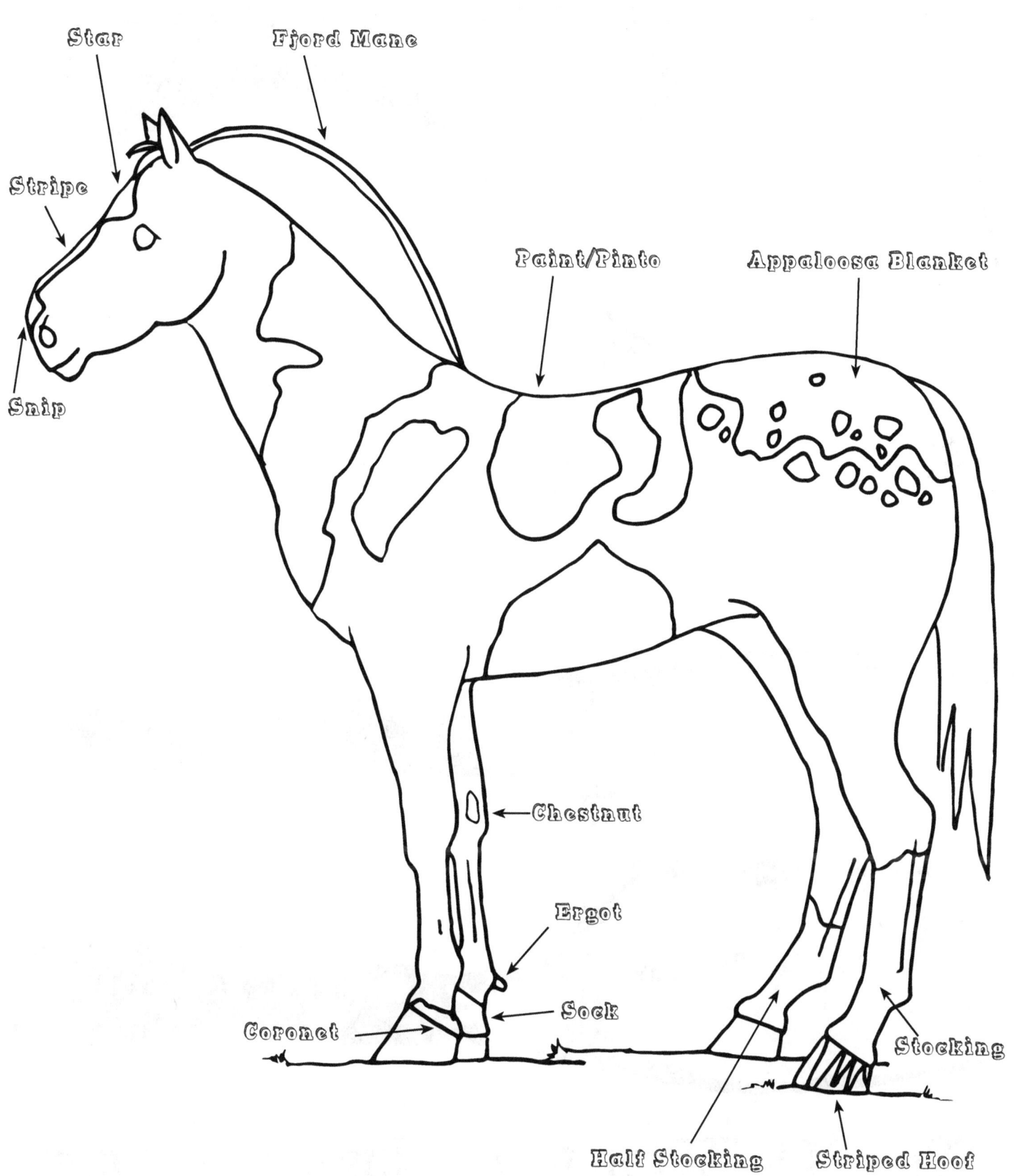

Horse Markings

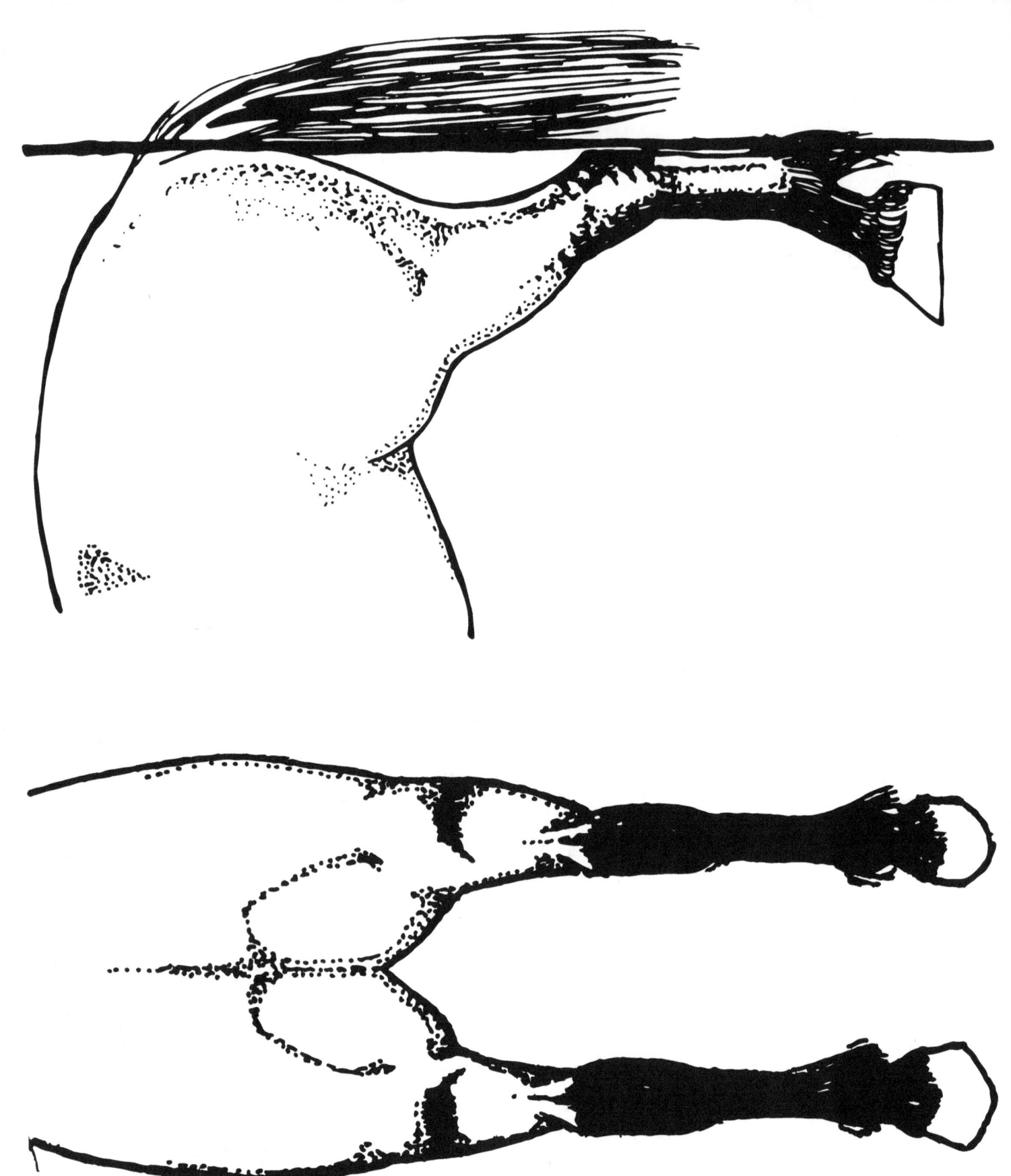

You'll Want to Know Good Conformation

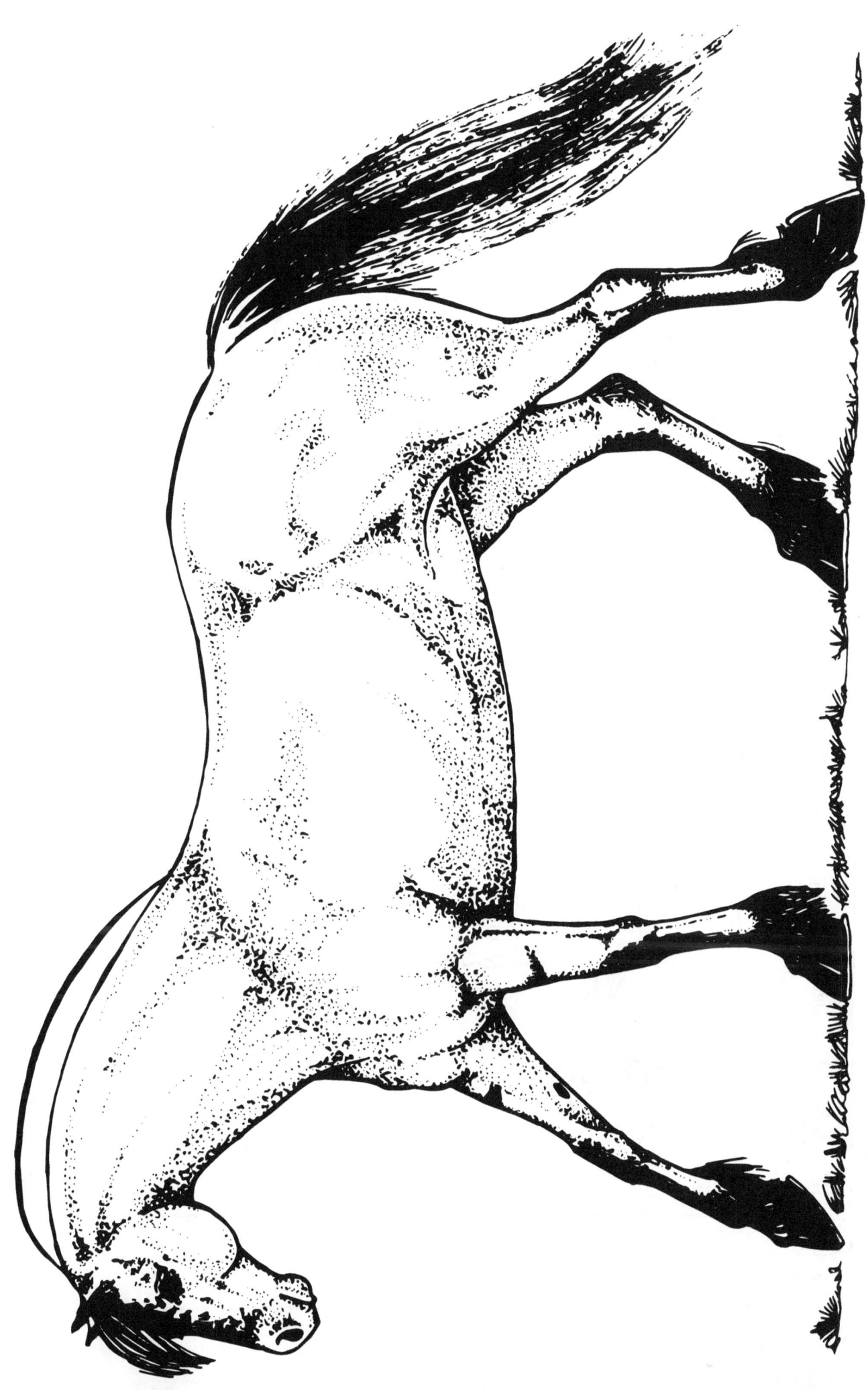

Collection is when a horse carries more weight on his hindlegs than his front legs. The horse draws the body in upon itself. **S**ometimes they need a little help.

FROM FRIENDS

Scores:
10 Excellent
9. Very Good
8. Good
7 Fairly good
6 Satisfactory
5 Insufficient
4 Fairly Bad
3 Bad
2. Very Bad
1 Not Executed
-1 Should be executed

5 lbs
10 lbs
15 lbs
20 lbs
50 lbs

DQ

HALF PASS
PASSAGE
PIAFFE
TEMPI CHANGES
PIROUETTES

PRIX ST GEORGES
INTERMEDIARE I
INTERMEDIARE II
GRAND PRIX

4TH LEVEL
3RD LEVEL
2ND LEVEL
1ST LEVEL
TRAINING
INTRO

WHERE IS C?
OH MY.
MISSION IMPOSSIBLE LEVEL
TRYING AGAIN Begin Over

HALT SALUTE
AT JUDGE'S TABLE.
J TO X

Don't Forget About Grooming

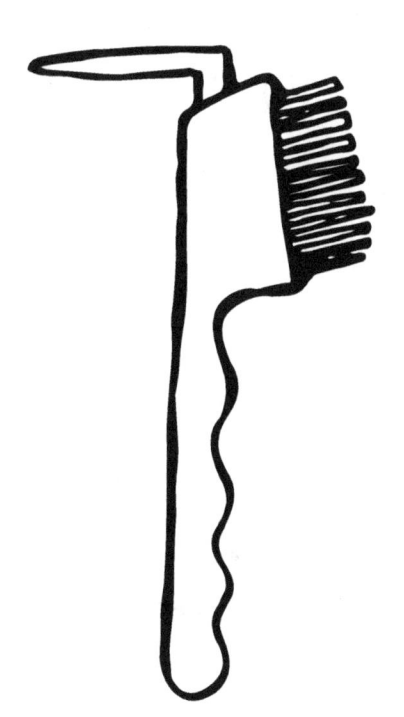

Hoof Pick

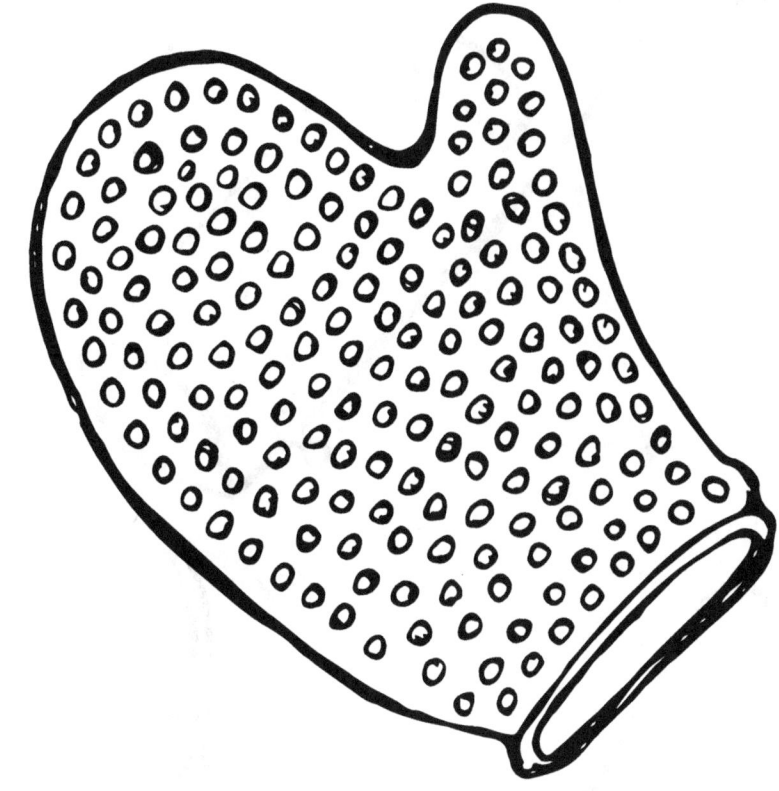

Mitt

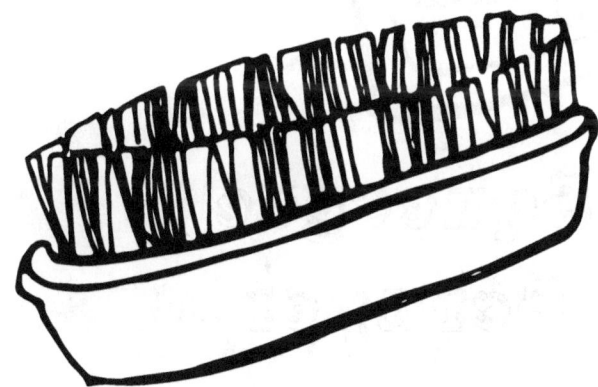

Brush

Curry Comb

Horse Grooming Tools

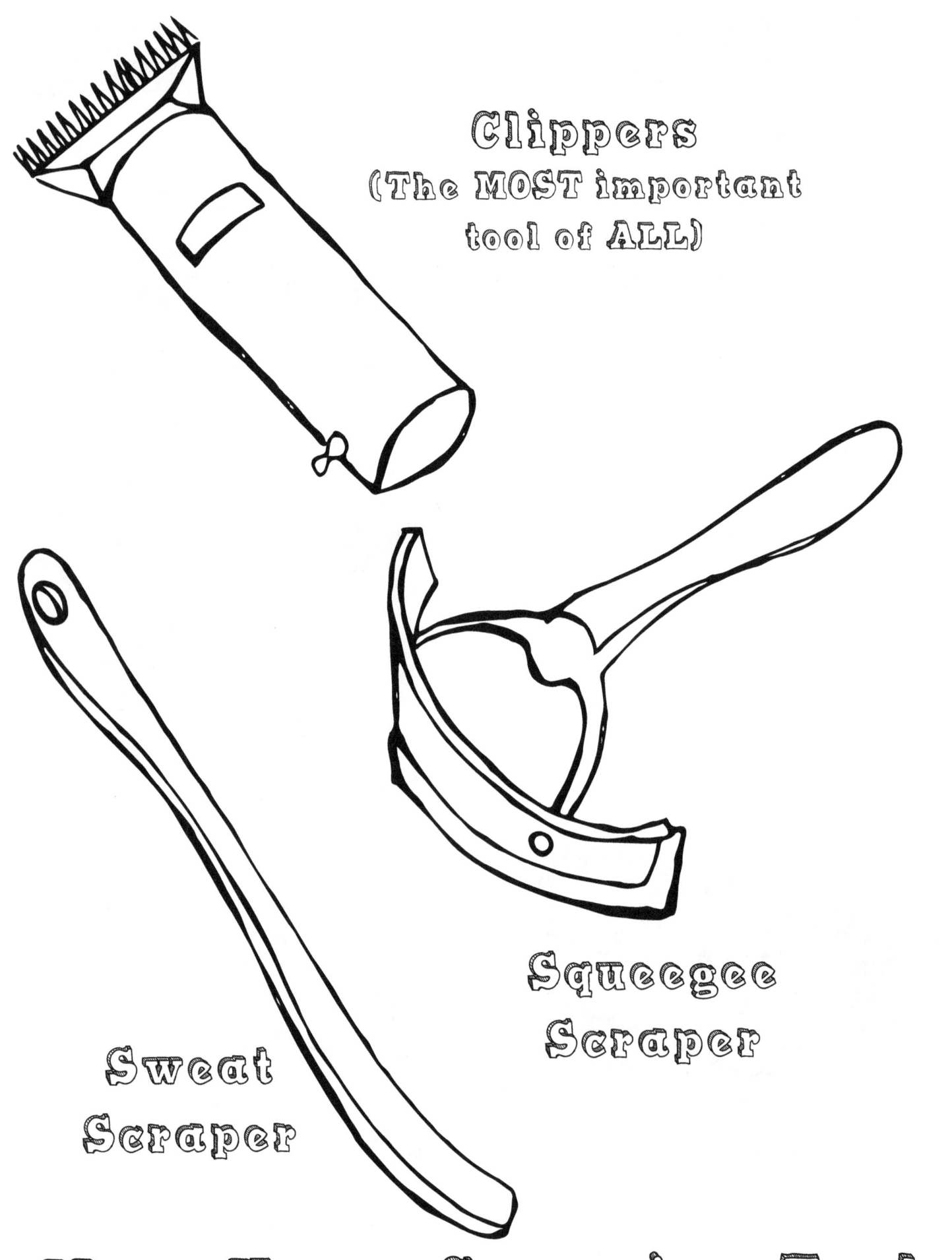

There's an Awful Lot to Learn and It Can Be Overwhelming

Learning Is Easier With Proper Instruction

You'll still make mistakes. And that's okay, because you can learn from them, too.

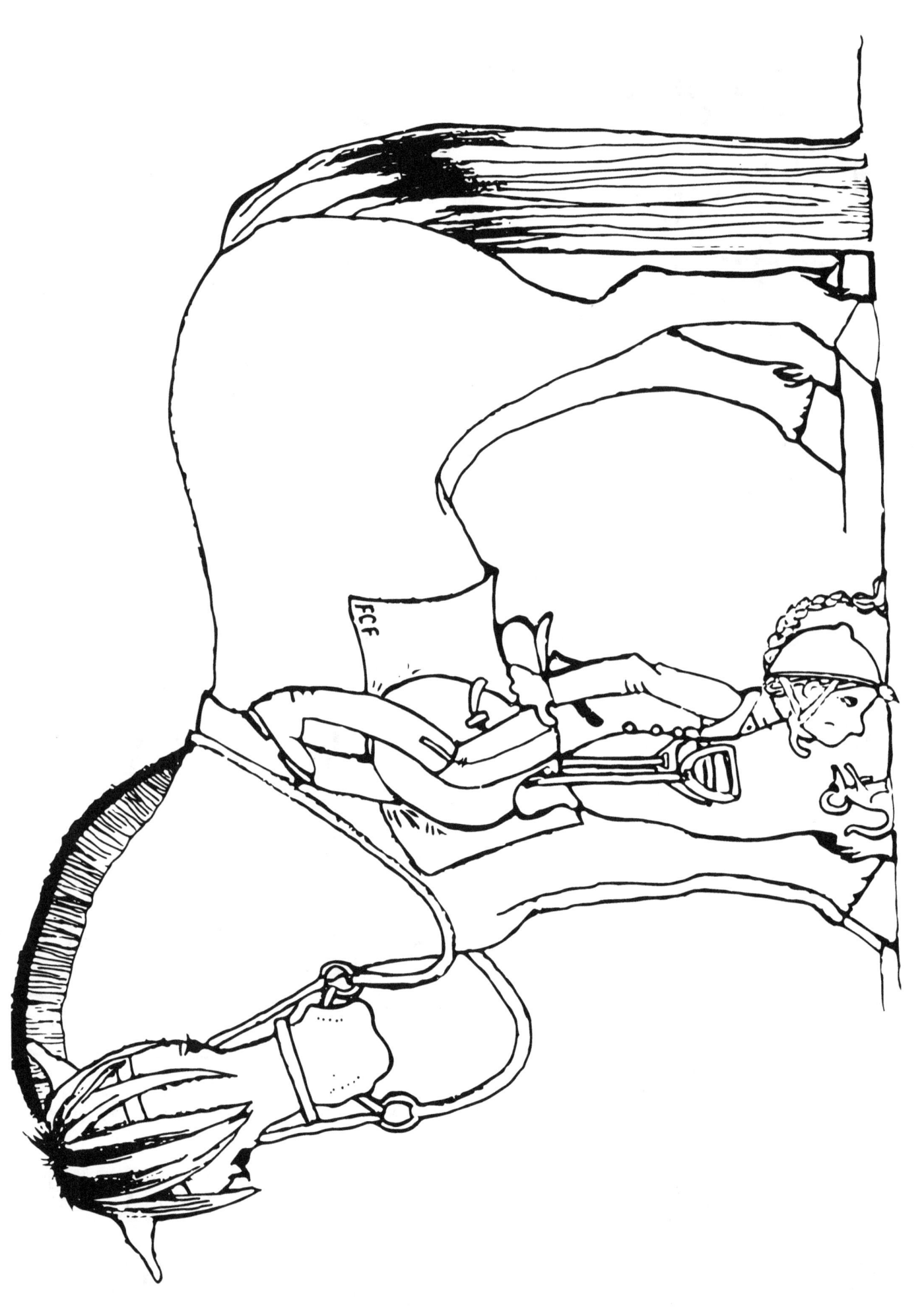

Even Horses Make Mistakes!

Fun Fjord Fact: People believe Fjord's tails and manes are spray-painted black. Nope. They're all natural.

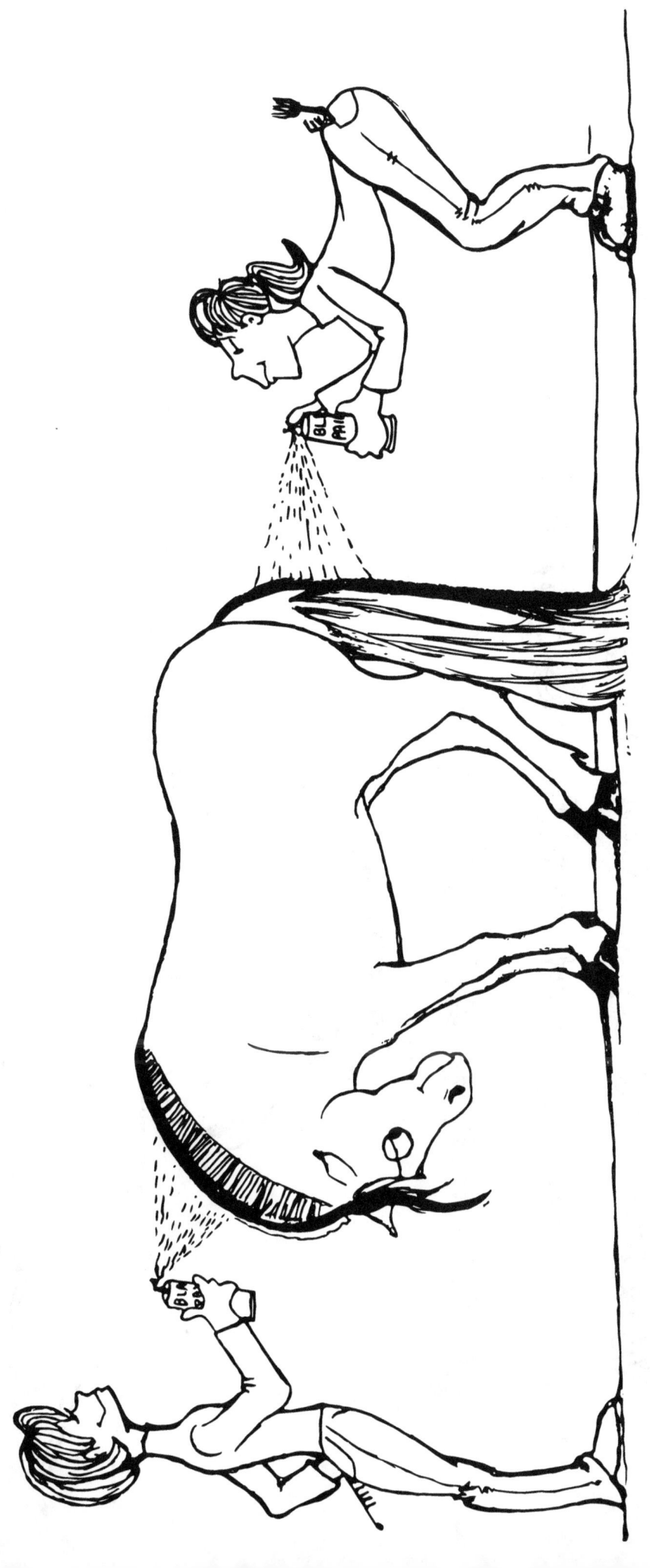

We're always working on new books! Write to us (fcfwalter@gmail.com) with your comments, ideas, or suggestions.

You might also like:

Color Your Way Into English Riding 2!

Color Your Way Into Western Riding!

and ...
Color Your Way Into Horseback Riding!
(includes English 1 & 2 and Western)

www.ingramcontent.com/pod-product-compliance
Lightning Source LLC
Chambersburg PA
CBHW080943040426

42444CB00015B/3434